The Busy Manager's Guide to Employee Relations Excellence

By:

John W. "Wes" Spence, CMC, SPHR

ISBN: 1-4107-7040-0 (e-book)
ISBN: 1-4107-7041-9 (Paperback)

Library of Congress Control Number: 2003094941

This book is printed on acid free paper.

Printed in the United States of America
Bloomington, IN

1stBooks - rev. 07/08/03

Dedication

Dedicated to all of the managers and employees

working together in the world of business,

with hopes that soon both groups will realize

that their goals are really not incompatible after all.

Special Thanks to

The Jeanne Bruce Company

Bruce Held and Jeanne Wood, Owners

P. O. Box 241, Bridge City, TX 77611

Editorial Consultants

Table of Contents

CHAPTER TWO

The Certified Employee Friendly Workplace

Introduction

Is this book going to be "pro-employee" or "pro-management"? The simple answer is—neither! This book is pro-*business*.

There is only one reason for doing anything in business and that is to make more money. Businesses can't afford the luxury of having both an employee agenda *and* a management agenda.

It is more difficult to defeat your competitors, introduce new products, and enter new markets while your resources are being consumed by conflicts between management and employees.

Why This Book Will Be Useful To You

This book focuses on usable steps that can be taken to improve your company's relationship with its employees. The solutions in this book are valid for both large and small businesses.

The core of this book is the punch-list of steps from my Certified Employee Friendly Workplace criteria, and an explanation of, and justification for, each step.

Show a sincere desire to identify problems and improve relationships, and your employees will boost productivity and profitability for the company.

Preface

(Or, What Gives Me the Right to Tell You about Employee Relations?)

I worked my way through college, and I consider my work experience my real education. I took management courses at night and worked during the day. I began to notice that at night school we were taught how things were supposed to be done, but all day at work the real world was quite different.

Deciding that the large utility company for which I worked must be "defective"; I left for a job with a huge natural gas pipeline company. The pay and benefits were better, but the relationship this company had with its employees was very bad. I spent the bulk of my 20-year telecommunication career with that company and had ample opportunity to analyze the problems.

Both of those companies were large and well known. They should have had employee relations down to an art. They did not.

I took a buy-out package from the pipeline company and accepted a position as an operations manager for a smaller company. It was enlightening to work on the management side of a company that did not know how to work effectively with its employees, for this one, too, had dreadful employee relations.

I got the real-world education of seeing those employee-hostile companies incur staggering costs and consequences. The more I saw of the results of poor employee relations practices, the more determined I was to become a management consultant.

As a consultant I have been able to help forward-looking and pro-active managers learn to have better relations with their employees. With a "been there and done that" background, I have had a high success rate. I know employee relations from the trenches. I have been an employee and I have been in management. I have seen how good employee relations practices can improve productivity, and I have seen bad employee relations bring a large company to its knees.

What I have learned can help you.

The Cost of Poor Employee Relations—A True Story

An out of town investor owned a small business but rarely visited. One day, employees saw him arrive. The investor went straight to the CEO's office and did not speak to or make eye contact with any of the employees he passed on the way in. After the meeting the investor left, still without acknowledging any of the employees he passed. The employees, who had no idea the investor had been expected, waited for some announcement about the meeting from the CEO.

It never came.

The usual operation of the business came to a near-halt as employees, feeling personally threatened, developed theories, and rumors spread.

The business was being sold.

All their jobs would be lost.

By the time management finally announced the meeting was routine and nothing negative would come of it, productivity and morale were at an all-time low and had to be rebuilt before normal activity resumed.

Understanding Good Employee Relations

By: Wes Spence, CMC, CEIP, SPHR

*Sometimes, to **really** understand a complex relationship, a new approach must be used. And so it is with the relationship between management and employees. In this article, a new approach is used to make employee relations easier to understand. This tool may also be useful to the reader in analyzing other processes within businesses.*

When I am in need of a tool to grasp a subject that is difficult to understand, I try to either blow it up to huge proportions or reduce it to its most basic terms. In employee relations, it is a known and proven fact that having a good relationship with employees is one of the key ingredients (*if not **the** key ingredient*) in having a successful business. "Treat your employees well and they will treat you well," "Keep employees informed and involved," "Employees should be trained to be of the highest use possible to the business," the list goes on. These statements are widely known, but their messages are not put to use in far too many businesses today. Managers may be distracted by the day-to-day operations of their business, they may have a perceived lack of resources to deal with employee relations challenges, or perhaps they are caught up in so-called "analysis paralysis." The best way to look at employee relations is to reduce the operation (for analysis purposes) to its most basic form: one person working alone at a table to produce your product. Better yet, let's say that one person *is* your business. The body/business receives raw material, processes it, and produces an output in the form of a finished product.

Here is an example: We all know that good management practice states that lines of communication must be open from the top down *and* bottom up. Most businesses have the top down working but have some difficulty with understanding why bottom up communication is also very important. If our body/business is working at its table and the central nervous system (management) commands it to pick up the first piece to the product and unknown to management the piece just came out of a high heat manufacturing process, the body *must* be able to quickly communicate that fact back to the central nervous system to release the part before the hand is damaged (production is lost). Too many businesses suffer from challenges that are widely known at the lower levels of the corporate ladder but management is often unaware of until too late (if at all).

Is this starting to make sense? Let's try another example: Extreme and constant restructuring seems to be a norm in business today. This would equate to removing the limbs and organs of our body/business to attempt to do more with less or adapt to a changing environment. Have things really changed that much that we can ignore the years of evolution that produced the body/business in its present form? Sometimes yes, but more often the answer is no. A layoff would be like cutting off an arm of our body/business because we feel it is no longer useful and it is consuming resources. Certainly there are cases in business as in medicine where the arm must be removed so that the rest of the body can survive, but too often in business it is a hasty and unnecessary decision that we would not consider if we were cutting off an actual arm. That arm might again be useful in the not so distant future and perhaps we do owe it a degree of loyalty for the years of service (not so much because it is the "right" thing to do, but because of the production damaging fear the other limbs will have that they may be cut next).

Some other examples might be to equate exercise for the body to the Japanese word *kaizen* that means slow constant improvement and has been used as a buzzword in management lore. Interpersonal conflict? That would equate to an arm and a leg at odds - not too hard to see what effects that would have on production in our model. Replacement of a CEO in a corporation would be like replacing the heart in our body/business model. Perhaps necessary, but do allow time for the new organs to start working together properly again. Use the body/business model to analyze solution scenarios before making a decision. Be sure actions are appropriate. I have seen Total Quality Management (TQM) programs attempted to be implemented in a business environment where more fundamental problems existed that needed resolution first. The employees revolted and undermined the TQM program because they saw it as it was, which was like doing a face-lift on a patient that really needed a heart transplant!

The bottom line is to carefully consider the big picture when making decisions in business. The body/business model should be helpful in many cases. Keep a strong focus on the only real reason to do *anything* in business and that is to make more money. It might be interesting to fantasize about what our body/business model could do if the body were a world-class athlete, but in the end isn't the real glory and respect reserved for those who did the best and went the farthest by efficiently using resources they had in the first place?

CHAPTER ONE

A Snapshot of Current Employee Relations

Issues and Changes

Shortages of Qualified Employees and Excessive

Turnover

An interesting issue in the employee relations and human resources field today is the shortage of qualified prospective employees to meet current demands. This is especially interesting when a news story appears one day about employee shortages at a company, and the very next news story reports another company is laying off hundreds, or thousands, of employees.

Obviously the key word here is qualified. The simplest answer is to train the workers you need, but that is not always cost effective. Therefore, if you see your company growing, be sure that any current employees who have demonstrated above average interests and abilities are given opportunities for training to prepare them to grow with the company. This will not only help you maintain a pool of qualified workers, but should have a motivational dimension as well.

A longer-term solution to the shortage is a partnering between business and educational institutions so graduates actually have knowledge, skills, and abilities employers want and will pay for. This practice should become more refined and more commonplace in the future.

The fastest and cheapest solution to shortages of employees is to minimize your company's turnover rate. Businesses can be devastated by excessive turnover. Your most qualified employees are the ones who can most easily find employment elsewhere and tend to do so when they see the first sign there may be problems affecting the future of the company. These are the very employees that you can least afford to loose. Ironically, the "problems" driving employees to leave may not actually exist and may only be <u>perceived</u> to be real. Such was the case with the mystery meeting between the investor and the CEO reported earlier in this book.

Employees know about "employment at will" laws, and hear news stories about mass layoffs. Job security means their families' survival. Whatever threatens their job threatens that survival. Strange activity in the workplace is threatening. Thus, it is vital to keep employees informed on company news. Even if the news is not positive, you can put the best "spin" on it. Rumor from the "grapevine" will have a much more negative flavor than anything learned through company communication. Keeping employees informed is a positive control on turnover.

Three other keys to controlling turnover are timely employee evaluations, employee surveys, and exit interviews. All three of these tools are effective if used correctly, but they are severely under-utilized in most businesses today.

Increasing numbers of women and minorities in the workforce is not a "problem." It is a change to be aware of and accommodate. Forward-looking companies will take advantage of the diversity this presents and abolish the "glass ceiling".

John W. "Wes" Spence, CMC, SPHR

Union Issues and Costly Labor Strikes

The major reason unions exist is poor management practices. None of us would have wanted to work under the conditions that the first unions were organized to combat. Unions in the U.S. have been losing ground since the 1950s or early 60s, but, unfortunately, many of the same management practices that led to their creation are still in use today. There are certainly examples of over-zealous unions and unreasonable demands, and to see companies brought to their knees by their unions is not pleasant. Recent costly labor strikes against well-known companies are examples of why unionization may not be in the best interest of your company. Unions are currently marketing themselves aggressively and efficiently.

If you already have a union at your company, there is still opportunity to develop a relationship with the union that minimizes the risk of strike. The Certified Employee Friendly

Workplace criteria introduced later in this book should give you a good start on maintaining a good working relationship with your employees whether or not a union is involved.

Mounting Concern About Job Security

This issue is complex and challenging. Obviously, many elements to this problem are out of the control of businesses and managers. Managers, however, should be aware of employee frustrations and take advantage of every means to eliminate the causes, or to diffuse the problems before they escalate and spread.

Personal issues your employees may have can be addressed helpfully through your company's Employee Assistance Program (EAP), if there is one. More EAP's are starting to offer expanded help on such matters as career counseling. Others offer assistance with problems such as alcohol and drug abuse.

To discover the causes of frustration and uneasiness with your employees as a group, use an employee opinion survey. Properly utilized, such employee opinion surveys can help identify obstacles interfering with your employees' productivity. If you do commit to doing an employee opinion survey, be willing to make some reasonable changes to overcome problems your employees identify for you. Otherwise your surveying efforts could cause an increase in frustration.

There is no reason to fear the results of an employee opinion survey. In my experience, the vast majority of issues that most frustrate employees and interfere with production are not difficult to overcome. It is certain that some problems exist within your company. Conducting a survey identifies problems that you may not otherwise learn about until a major problem has developed. Used correctly, an employee opinion survey is a powerful tool which empowers managers to find and correct problems at an early stage.

Open and honest communication with employees is essential to alleviate frustration and uneasiness.

Increase in Employee Violence

Supervisor conflicts, non-productive co-workers, fear of the unknown, and changes in the business routine which may personally affect employees are major causes of unease. If those issues continue to exist and compound, employees feel helpless and out of control.

Workforce violence stories are favorites in the news media these days. Coverage focuses on disgruntled former employees. However, some statistics released by OSHA indicate the media emphasizes the least dangerous sector. Workplace violence is perpetrated 44% by customers and clients, 24% by strangers, 20% by co-workers, 7% by bosses, and only 3% by former employees.

Overall Worsening of Management / Employee Relations

A Golden Rule attitude in dealing with conflicts is the key to handling most of them.

A clear system of due process is essential.

Training first-line supervisors in conflict resolution can help.

A true story will illustrate:

A young employee believed that if he treated the company right, then he would be treated right. He was the only employee in his department that did not abuse the generous expense account allowances. He felt that the company's expense policy was lenient and allowed him to eat and sleep well on business trips. Something happened to change his opinion of the company.

At an annual department meeting, the head of the department explained he made a fantastic discovery. While the employee handbook stated that employees would be eligible for merit raises annually, the manual did not define what <u>annual</u> actually meant! It did not specify 365 days, the approximate time it takes the Earth to go around the Sun. The manager, beaming with enthusiasm at his revelation, announced from that day on, <u>annual</u> would mean something different for each different employee. For some, annual would be nine months, and for others it could be as high as 23 months! That got the attention of the audience because it would impact their paychecks.

The young employee had his annual term arbitrarily set at 15 months. This practice was not done to correct inequalities in pay scales. There was truly no legitimate reason!

The employee took out a calculator and figured out how much money this strange practice would cost him. He added that amount, plus interest, to his expense account until it was all paid back.

Joke as we may, two wrongs really do not make a right.

There is a very important message here to managers. If your employees <u>feel</u> that they have been mistreated, they will find a way to get you back! This is true and unavoidable. To make matters worse, the mistreatment may just be a <u>perception</u> of mistreatment when a legitimate action is taken by management but misunderstood by employees. If the employees <u>feel</u> that they were wronged, the results will be the same.

Remember, your employees understand the operation of your business very well. They know where to put the torpedo to do the most damage. In a management / employee dispute, everyone suffers.

When an action <u>may</u> be misunderstood by the employees, every effort should be made to explain the action and eliminate the possibility of misunderstanding. It is vitally important that managers learn to think through how employees may perceive, or misperceive, changes. They must keep asking employees for their input and comments. Do this until a climate of trust exists between the management and the employees. Then keep doing it.

Humans tend to respond to conflict by digging in rather than working out differences and problems. Disagreement between management and employees can result in labor strikes, resignations, sabotage, and lawsuits. The best corporate cultures will provide an environment that seeks to solve small problems before they get to be big problems.

Increasing Numbers of Employee Lawsuits Against Employers

When Congress passes regulations governing businesses and employees, enforcement is assigned to the department of the government Congress feels is most appropriate to manage it. Practical details are often left unaddressed.

Your Human Resources person or department should be your first line of defense.

Some businesses have chosen to minimize lawsuits with alternative dispute resolution (ADR) programs. When a company has an ADR program in place, there is a procedure to follow to reach resolution. Suing the company is not an alternative.

Some large corporations are starting to require JDs (law degrees) as a qualification for HR Director. This is not the proper focus for a business that is interested in preventing lawsuits in the first place. If your company does use a JD for an HR Director, be sure to balance that person with another high level HR person concentrating on employee issues.

MBFQ

Managing By the Fiscal Quarter has been an unfortunate outcome of the wild ride the stock market has given investors in recent years. Corporate executives and entrepreneurs, sensitive to fluctuations in stock price, try to protect the share value of the company's stock at all times and at all costs. The bottom line is that there is an over-emphasis on fiscal quarters and an under-emphasis of longer-term outlooks in management today. Many of the most important tasks facing business today can not provide a pay-off within one fiscal quarter, but will be rewarding in the longer term.

MADness

By "MAD" I am referring to Mergers, Acquisitions, and Downsizing. These practices "enhance shareholder value" for the short-term while often allowing the company to suffer in the longer term. The great majority of employee relations problems during these periods stem from lack of proper communication with employees to let them know what is going on and how it might affect them.

Downsizing is not always the answer. Your employees are seeing the actual problems that are plaguing your business every day. Let them identify those problems and suggest ways of overcoming them. Find a creative and cost-effective way of rewarding them for their help.

Increasing Legal Requirements and Restrictions by Government Agencies

In many ways this situation, like the unionization issue, is self-inflicted by some managers who operate unfairly, take advantage of situations, and push existing laws to the maximum at the expense of others.

A true story will illustrate this:

A smaller business was looking for any possible way to increase profits. This business had a 401(k) plan for their employees. The managers determined that if they took the deductions out of their employees' checks on time, but held on to the money in an interest bearing account until the last possible legal minute, they could make free money on the "float". This was legal since they usually did get the money to the plan administrators before the law was violated.

On the surface, the scheme seemed to work. They did make a little extra money. But there were two fundamental problems. First, they made this money at the expense of their employees. If the money HAD been deposited in the employees' accounts on time, the *employees* would have been earning gains on it instead of the company. After all, part of the money was taken from the employees' checks in the first place.

The second problem is that the company demonstrated in their corporate culture it is perfectly all right to push rules and laws to the limit for personal or corporate gain. So the employees learned to push company rules, such as personal use of company vehicles, to the maximum and beyond. That is the way they were trained. The relatively small amount of interest the company made on the float was hardly worth the price they had to pay for it.

The law now requires that such money be deposited in retirement accounts on a more timely basis. Legitimate companies that previously had the option to use delayed deposits to overcome short-term cash flow problems no longer have that option. All companies are forced to endure yet another regulation because some companies chose to take unfair advantage of a situation.

CHAPTER TWO

The Certified Employee Friendly Workplace

A one-stop listing of steps to create and maintain a good working relationship with employees.

Why certified? Companies committed to excellent employee relations could be identified by displaying the CEFW certificate.

Certification is awarded on a points system on three levels: Small-Sized Company (1-100 employees), Medium-Sized Company (101-500 employees), and Large-Sized Company (over 500 employees). Numbers determining a company's level can be adjusted to fit specific circumstances.

The criteria for each are listed here. While all criteria are important, clearly some are imperative. A management consultant can address specific issues and offer some leeway in criteria to be met for certification.

A company which meets the criteria is an employee friendly workplace. That is, of course, the goal. There is, therefore, a value in a visible symbol which would publicly declare that the company has made the effort and has achieved the criteria.

The Certified Employee Friendly Workplace Small-Sized Company Criteria List

1.   Hold an employee orientation for each new employee. This should include an employee handbook, organizational chart, and a discussion of procedures and expectations.

2.   Give a progress review of each new employee at a date one-month from the hire date to discuss how he or she is doing and to answer any questions.

3.   Keep all employees informed on the longer-range goals and mission statement of the company.

4. Conduct employee opinion surveys at intervals not to exceed three years. Post results of the surveys for all employees to see.

5. Conduct employee evaluations of all employees at intervals not to exceed one year.

6. Implement a due process for handling employee/supervisor disputes and complaints. Distribute the procedure in writing to each employee. In addition, an open door policy or managed open door policy is recommended to give employees access to higher levels of management.

7. Proactively maintain a cooperative attitude toward employee issues and demonstrate it by both words and deeds

8. Formally designate at least one person as having the duties and responsibilities of a Human Resources Department. That person can hold other position(s) at the same time.

9. Assure that wages and benefits generally meet or exceed those of other companies in the same industry and the same size.

10. Agree to meet or exceed compliance with all of the laws and regulations that are required of the business as they apply to employees.

11. Agree to eliminate all types of discrimination and harassment in the workplace. Policies to that effect should be written in the employee handbook.

12. Conduct exit interviews on all employees leaving the company. The results of those interviews will be reviewed by higher levels of management.

13. Post job openings within the company where employees will easily see them. Procedures will be in place for "bidding" on those jobs.

The Certified Employee Friendly Workplace

Medium-Sized Company Criteria List

Meet or exceed all criteria for small-sized company certification and include the following modifications:

1.   Have at least one full-time Human Resources Person.

2.   Conduct employee opinion surveys at intervals not to exceed two years. Post results as in small company criteria.

Additionally:

3.   The organization shall have a formalized system for handling employee suggestions. This system does not have to be elaborate or reward employees for suggestions. There should be some form of timely feedback to the employees who do make suggestions.

4.   The organization shall have some form of retirement for employees. This can be as simple as a 401(k) plan with a minimum of 30% matching of the employee contribution, or a more generous retirement plan.

5.   The organization shall produce and distribute to all employees an organizational newsletter for the purpose of enhancing communications with employees and to help them better understand the relevant issues and activities of the organization. This newsletter is to be produced at least quarterly, and may be distributed by electronic means.

6.   Evaluate the training needs of the employees at least yearly and provide needed training as conditions and budgets permit.

7.   Have at least 80% of employees agree that the organization is truly "employee friendly". This can be done most efficiently as a question on the employee survey.

8.   It is suggested, but not required for certification, that wage increases for employees are tied to issues relating to their individual performance and not just longevity. It is recognized that this will not be possible in unionized environments.

The Certified Employee Friendly Workplace Large-Sized Company Criteria List

Meet or exceed all criteria for both small-sized and medium-sized company levels with the following modifications:

1.   Conduct employee opinion surveys annually unless otherwise justified.

2.   Provide at least a 50% match to employee retirement fund contributions.

3.   Increase the employee involvement (suggestion) program to at least an intermediate level with a designated contact person responsible for the

administration of the program. That contact person may hold other position(s) at the same time. Participation in the program should be at least 30% of eligible employees.

4. Have some type of gain-sharing plan with employees. This is subject to affordability and participation. Temporary suspension in times of organizational hardship will be allowed.

5. Provide training over a reasonable time frame to at least all first and second line supervisors on the subjects of workplace diversity, prevention of harassment, conducting proper evaluations of employees, and other issues as deemed necessary. Such needs may be indicated by employee survey results, exit interviews, or incidents of related employee complaints. This training may be conducted by company personnel.

6. Quality of Work Life (QWL) assessments shall be performed and reported to upper management at periods not to exceed three years. This assessment is

to be considered a report card as to how company policies have served to enhance the quality of the organization as a place to work.

7.   It is suggested, but not required for certification, that the organization adopt some type of Alternative Dispute Resolution (ADR) program to protect itself and minimize distractions from employee litigation while still maintaining a fair and reasonable means of resolving the more serious conflicts.

8.   It is suggested, but not required, that the companies allow comp-time in lieu of overtime pay for employees who want it. This is, of course, subject to current and pending labor laws and union agreements.

John W. "Wes" Spence, CMC, SPHR

Explanations and Reasoning behind the CEFW for

Small-Sized Companies

Employee Orientation

When you hire the best-qualified candidate and follow all of the laws and restrictions on hiring, can you afford to do less than to make sure that the newly hired employee gets off to the best possible start? Having a good employee orientation program is a key to avoiding problems in the future.

Write out and communicate company policies and procedures to all employees. Employee handbooks are excellent tools for such communications. When you give out an employee handbook, you should have each employee sign a document stating he or she <u>has</u> read and understands the information in the handbook and put that document in his personnel file.

Employee handbooks are just the beginning of an effective employee orientation program. New employees need to know how their job relates to the company as a whole and how their job makes a contribution to what the company does and why it is important. Give the new employees a written job description and an organizational chart. Show them where they are on the chart to let them begin to understand the big picture. Tell them the names of their boss's boss and his or her boss. That could save some confusion when there is a crisis and the new employees' supervisors are not available.

If your new employees will be responsible for completing monthly or weekly paperwork, give them lists of the due dates to allow them to plan for prompt completion.

Employees' orientation does not have to be extensive or lengthy. But it must get them started well and let them know where to go to get questions answered. Orientation is the time to give explanations for rigid rules or procedures. Answer any questions. In short, do anything and everything possible to make the new employee's beginning with your company positive and productive. This beginning will form an impression of the company that may last for the length of his employment with you.

Why not just let new employees ask a co-worker? A disgruntled employee is often the first co-worker to welcome your new employees. Disgruntled employees are always looking for allies, and the conversation begins with, "Let me tell you how it really is around here..."

Starting the new employee off with a positive experience is crucial.

One Month Progress Review

A review with the new employee on the one-month anniversary of his or her hire date does not have to be written or intense. Just get him into a relaxed environment and ask how things are going. This process could take 15 minutes to an hour. Give him one more chance to ask questions now that he has been exposed to the job for some time. Be sure that questions or concerns are answered or followed up on promptly. Remember, your employee is judging and forming an opinion of the company during this period, so make sure it is a good one. If your company considers newly hired employees temporary for a set period of time, and/or the employee is not working out too well, this review should be written and kept in the personnel file.

A true story may illustrate new employee orientation:

I was hired by a large company to operate as a solo employee responsible for the operation of a large area in two states. When I was hired, I was shown where the business locations were but not given any clues on how or when to complete the large amount of paperwork I was responsible for. I was told to "just ask someone."

Since I did not have any personal contact with my co-workers, I would telephone to ask questions, rotating through the list so as not to overburden any of them, or look too stupid. My co-workers weren't sure when or how to do the paperwork, either. I got conflicting due dates and routing procedures even though we all answered to the same supervisor. There were serious managerial and operational problems with the department.

My opinion of that company, formed by that experience and realization, stayed with me for the entire time I was employed there.

Company Goals and Mission Statement

The mission statement and general long-range goals of your organization must be clearly communicated to all employees. Communicating can be as simple as posting them, neatly framed, on a wall in clear view in an area employees frequent. Company upper management must support and believe in the goals and mission statement if they are to have meaning to your employees.

Some companies have required employees to memorize goals and/or mission statements. This develops resentment, so unless there is some legitimate reason for it, this is not advisable.

Communicating goals to employees lets them know and understand where the company is trying to go. That knowledge will pay dividends when your employees are able to make some decisions on their own. Keep the goals attainable and missions doable; these are legitimate business tools and not a corporate wish list.

Employee Opinion Surveys

Employee opinion surveys are probably the most powerful tools available today in employee relations work. Done correctly, these instruments are inexpensive and yield a wealth of useful information. Employee surveying has been a core service of my management consulting practice for years, and I know how to make them pay off.

Problems are best handled when they are small. Employee surveys identify small problems before they have a chance to become big problems.

If you ask your employees for their input and do not use it, employees will feel their trust was violated and that management feels employees have nothing worthwhile to contribute. Employees expect some action to be taken on the survey results, but they do not expect major changes just because they wish it.

Managers should not look at the results of an employee survey as an avalanche of new problems that they have to solve. Extremely negative survey results are actually quite rare. Employees respond very well to surveys, and many of the problems are easy to solve. Once you get the survey results tabulated, post the results for the employees to see and tell them, "Thanks for the help. Now, how are we going to solve these challenges?". Let them offer solutions to the problems that they identified. This will free the managerial staff from the entire responsibility of solving all of the new problems.

Outside consultants can handle employee surveying more effectively than internal staff, since employees feel more confident their identities will be kept confidential. Outside consultants are usually more cost-effective as well.

If you get only mediocre results from your first employee survey, go with the information they did give and make earnest efforts to address the issues. The next time your employees are surveyed they will be more forthcoming.

Employee Evaluations

Each employee must be formally reviewed by his or her supervisor at least annually. This review should be an objective review of the employee's performance of job duties, as well as an honest review of the employee's interpersonal relationships with co-workers and others. The review should then be approved by the supervisor's boss. Should the employee not agree with the review, further discussions with the supervisor and the supervisor's boss shall be held until the matter is resolved. A written policy for reaching resolution should be in the employee handbook.

Due Process

When people work together, there will be conflicts. Due process for handling conflicts fairly and efficiently is essential for a smoothly running organization. How the conflicts were handled will be remembered long after the reasons for the conflicts are forgotten.

Should a disagreement reach an impasse, a due process procedure should be available. An example of such an impasse would be a disagreement between a supervisor and a subordinate in which the subordinate refuses to accept the supervisor's ruling. Without a due process procedure, the subordinate is left with no options other than to take the matter to the next level of supervision over his or her boss's head, or to sue the company. Both of those solutions are unacceptable.

Alternative Dispute Resolution (ADR) programs may be helpful to your organization.

So-called Open-door Policies in which any employee is free to see anyone in management whenever he wants to may be helpful in some situations. A Managed Open-door Policy will serve better, in which employees are still allowed access to management, but only after going through the chain-of-command or by scheduling an appointment with the manager in advance. Open door policies can be a burden on managers' time and cause chain-of-command violations and challenges. In a situation where a supervisor and subordinate can not agree on a matter, it would not be helpful for the subordinate to take the problem to the company president without trying other methods of resolution first. Moreover, any ruling would create more problems.

Having a due process procedure is the solution. Due process, done correctly, will minimize employee lawsuits and maintain fairness and cordial employee relations.

John W. "Wes" Spence, CMC, SPHR

Top Management's Attitude toward Employees

If your organization wants to be known and certified as being truly employee friendly, top management will have to show commitment to that attitude. It will not suffice for management to <u>say</u> they are committed to good employee relations and not <u>show</u> it. I have never seen a managerial team that could consistently fool their employees into thinking they were employee friendly when they were not. Your employees watch you more than you can imagine and they know when they are being fooled. If your organization has had a history of poor employee relations, it will take longer for employee trust to be reestablished, but it is doable. Just regain their trust one deed at a time, the way you lost it. Once the employees see that you are serious and committed, they will come to trust you again.

Examine company policy to eliminate any employee hostile elements.

One large company had a policy that any car accidents in company vehicles were automatically the fault of the employee—unless the company vehicle was legally parked. Any "safety violations" would remain in the employees' personnel files and would be considered negatively during promotion reviews. The policy was easy to administer, since no accidents needed investigation, but it was unmistakably employee hostile.

Formally Designated Human Resources Person

In today's complex business environment, the HR function even for small businesses is very important. At least one person must be responsible for it. That person is your central focus point for all HR matters. If the job is shared unofficially by several employees, the organization will not have any consistency and many important duties will be allowed to slip. For the purpose of small company CEFW certification, that person can still hold other positions at the same time. The point is to have at least one person who is responsible to see that HR matters are tended to. As the company grows and more employees and HR duties are added, this person should probably be made a full-time human resources person. Continually updating the training of your HR person is highly recommended.

Wages and Benefits

For certification purposes, all that is required is that the wages and benefits generally meet or exceed those of similar sized businesses in similar industries. The vast majority of organizations that wish to certify as employee friendly should have no problem qualifying here. There are many sources for information on wages and benefits.

Compliance with Employee Laws and Regulations

Like the wage and benefit section above, this should not be a stumbling block for reasonably well-run businesses. Organizations operating outside legal guidelines and regulations would certainly not be interested in being called employee friendly. It is perhaps best to look upon the laws and restrictions as tools to help you keep your business out of trouble and incentives for always trying to treat employees fairly.

Discrimination and Harassment

Many laws and regulations cover discrimination and harassment. This area is a hotbed of legal action. Modern management must be pro-active in this area to minimize the risk of legal problems.

As our society gets more diverse and more complicated, it is natural that business relations will be affected. If you feel you are particularly at risk in this area, there are a variety of consultants available to audit your business procedures and practices and offer advice for improvements. See *Institute of Management Consultants* in Part Three. Once the proper controls and safeguards are in place, this area of risk can be quite manageable.

Exit Interviews

As is the case with employee surveys, exit interviews can be very useful if done correctly. It is unfortunate that in most businesses today, exit interviews are either not done at all or are half-heartedly done. This is your last chance to get any useable information from an outgoing employee. Exit interviews are so important; they should even be given to employees being fired. The latter may not be cooperative, but if one useful piece of information comes from the effort, it is worth it. Exit interview results have also been successfully used to defeat "constructive discharge" law suits.

Exit interviews should be done with care and designed so that maximum data will be obtained. Furthermore, the results should be seen by higher levels of management. This provides them with information on why turnover is occurring and will provide an additional system of checks and balances to uncover any supervisors that are causing unwanted turnover. Let your employees know that these exit interviews are viewed by upper management as very important tools and any information on them is taken seriously.

Posting of Job Openings

It is very important that your upwardly mobile employees receive timely information on positions available within the company. There are many reasons to do this. From an equal opportunity angle, you certainly want to be able to tell any government investigators that all openings are posted or distributed and all employees have access. You do not want to give any impression to your employees that you are keeping openings secret from them or restricting access because that would violate the atmosphere of cooperation that you are trying to establish.

Employees going back to school obviously are looking for a better position and may be more valuable to your company. I have actually witnessed a large company that paid for college tuition for employees, but gave them no access to intra-company job openings. Each employee in turn got a degree and left the company. The co-workers all understood what was happening. Unfortunately, management did not. The sad solution that management came up with was to not hire anyone that was going or thinking about going back to school!

Just because you post the jobs for the employees to see, there is certainly no reason that a more qualified individual can not be hired from the outside. The only warning here is to be sure that you do focus on the most qualified. If a more qualified outsider is hired over an existing employee, there may be some disappointment but there will rarely be a challenge. If the employees never hear about openings until they are filled, there are possibilities for all sorts of problems such as discrimination charges from minorities who never hear about the openings.

Explanations and Reasoning behind the CEFW for Medium-Sized Companies

Medium-sized company certification should be in reach of medium sized and more progressive small-sized businesses. As your business grows and becomes more complicated, you may find that many of the criteria listed here are already in place due to necessity.

Organizations seeking medium-sized company certification must meet all of the criteria for small company level with the following two modifications:

Full-time Human Resources Person

There must be at least one full-time person to handle the Human Resources and Employee Relations duties. This will most likely already be in place due to necessity and risk avoidance. By the time an organization grows to mid-size, the HR duties usually become so complex that a full-time HR person is hired. If you hire a competent person for this position, your investment should pay you back many times over as problems are prevented.

Employee Opinion Surveys

For medium-sized company certification, the interval of the employee surveys must not exceed two years. In reality, if your business and/or its environment are changing at a pace that is considered normal, you may find that you need to survey annually. Once you do your first employee survey, the next one will give you very valuable feedback on how your solutions to the challenges uncovered in the first one are going. Once you get your organization on a constant improvement track, it starts to work like compound interest with each gain you make multiplying all that went before. It is very powerful.

In addition, the following criteria have been added for medium-sized company CEFW:

Formalized System for Handling Employee Suggestions

A formalized system for handling employee suggestions does not have to be elaborate or costly. The reason for formalizing the system is so the organization can receive maximum benefit with minimum conflicts. Conflicts occur in suggestion systems when prizes are awarded and/or egos are involved. There need to be processes in place so that employees receive timely feedback on suggestions, and so that implementation of approved suggestions is accomplished within a reasonable time. Nothing will irritate employees more than making a suggestion and seeing it die waiting for approval or implementation.

Employee suggestion systems add to the idea that all of your employees help you run your organization better. If you want to get a good start on a suggestion system and not spend time reinventing the wheel, there are some excellent resources available. The first is called "I-Power." I-Power is a system developed by Martin Edelston of Boardroom, Inc. There is a book called <u>I-Power, The Secrets of Great Business in Bad Times,</u> written by Martin Edelston and Marion Buhagiar. I believe it is the simplest system for handling employees' suggestions. Boardroom, Inc. runs I-Power seminars in various locations throughout the year. See Greenwich Institute for American Education and the Employee Involvement Association (EIA) in Part Three of this book.

Employee Retirement Plan

By the time an organization reaches the point that CEFW medium level is desired, there is a high chance this requirement has already been met. The criteria calls for at least a 401(k) or 403(b) type plan with a minimum of 30% employer matching. With the competition of today's labor market, most likely your organization already offers such a plan or something better.

Allowances are made for temporary suspension of employer contributions during times of crisis, and the requirement is subject to modifications as regulations change.

Company Newsletter

Having a company newsletter can be a great asset to your organization. Used correctly, this newsletter can get important news to your employees and put the proper spin and fanfare to keep employees informed and focused on what good things the organization is up to. A newsletter is not to be used as a propaganda tool for the company. The information should be factual, because if not, the employees will disregard and laugh-off any information it contains.

Be sure to use your newsletter to report organizational news and activities, but also add a human dimension to it with more personal news such as employee marriages and newborns.

You are also encouraged to take questions relevant to business operations from employees and answer them in the newsletter. If you do take questions, answer truthfully, even if you do not put the company in the best possible light. Edit out any improper questions or those relating to secret operations such as merger talks.

Your organization should produce a newsletter at least quarterly and distribute it to all employees. Electronic distribution is encouraged where possible.

Employee Training

Training your workforce is vital and highly recommended. However, for certification purposes, the requirement is only that training be provided and evaluated as conditions and budgets permit.

It is a sad fact that training programs are often among the first to be cut as budgets contract. It is much more reasonable to run your organization with a constant eye on reducing costs. That way, there is minimal disruption when your markets take a downturn or competition increases. In other words, you have broken the feast-and-famine cycle and chosen a path in between.

The training you provide should be relevant to your employees' duties and there should always be a payback for the training. Employees should be more valuable to the organization after training than before. One way to help assure that is to make up an employee feedback form to be used after any training is given. Stay away from such questions as "Was the training enjoyable?". Focus on actual improvements in knowledge, skills and abilities. Ask the employees what they learned that will help them in their jobs. Ask if they would suggest this training for other employees. Remind them that the company provides training as a tool to increase production and save money. When the training is cost-effective, it is good for both the employees and the company.

Employee Friendly Acid Test

This part of the medium-sized company CEFW criteria states that 80% of your employees must agree that your organization can be considered employee friendly. This point was not added to give stress to managers. It was added as an acid test that the organization is truly demonstrating in word and deed an attitude of mutual respect and win-win actions when dealing with employees. It could be possible that an organization follow the letter of the CEFW criteria, but not the meaning. Employee Friendly Certification is not meant to be a test; it is meant to be a reward for doing what is right for both your organization and your employees.

There seems to be an epidemic of employees not trusting the management of their companies. Employees do not feel that management has the company's best interest in mind, and they feel the management is not particularly competent. In so many of these cases, management has done nothing to deserve that opinion. For this reason, the CEFW criteria were created as a tool to improve that situation. An employee approval rating as stated above should be easily reachable if your company is really following the spirit of employee friendliness. The easiest way to take this poll is with your scheduled employee survey.

Wage Increases

It is suggested, but not required for certification, that wage increases for employees be tied to issues relating to their individual performance in their jobs, and not just longevity. Of course, if your organization is unionized, this most likely can not be done.

Meetings to discuss employee wage increases should not be held at the same time as employee evaluations. A vast majority of organizations do them at the same time. What happens when there is some type of downturn in business and wages must be temporarily frozen? In that case, an outstanding employee could receive a great evaluation and the entire experience negated by the next sentence where he or she is told that there will be no corresponding wage increase. If evaluations and pay reviews are done at the same time, your employees think of them as the same thing. Your best employees should, of course, receive the highest pay increases as a reward and example to others. But tying wages and evaluations together is a potential problem.

Explanations and Reasoning behind the CEFW for Large-Sized Companies

The highest level of achievement in the CEFW program is the large-sized company level. It is intended for larger corporations or other organizations which have extremely valuable employees and competition for those employees is fierce. As with the other levels, there is nothing in the large company level that should place unreasonable demands on the organization. As with the other levels, organizations seeking to certify at this level must meet or exceed all of the criteria for the other levels with the following modifications:

Employee Opinion Surveys

Employee opinion surveys must be conducted every twelve months unless otherwise justified to be too often.

John W. "Wes" Spence, CMC, SPHR

Retirement Plan

The employer matching for whatever retirement program you have chosen is to be at a level of no less than 50% of employee contributions. As before, this matching can be suspended in times of hardship for the organization.

Employee Involvement Program

The employee involvement program is to be increased to at least an intermediate level with a designated contact person for that program. That contact person is allowed to hold other position(s) at the same time. Employee participation in the employee involvement program is to be no less than 30% of eligible employees.

In Addition, the following criteria have been added for large-sized company CEFW:

Gain-Sharing Plan

An organization operating at this level should have some type of gain sharing plan for employees. Non-profit organizations and others in financial hardship are exempt from this. Gain sharing should not be looked upon as an unreasonable burden to the organization's cash flow. You are simply offering the employees a piece of the gains that they help bring about. Normally, gain-sharing programs are designed in such a way that the sharing does not begin until a set level is reached. That level should not be impossible, but should require obvious extra effort and take the organization to a level that would, most likely, not have been attainable without the additional incentives.

First- and Second-Line Supervisor Training

Due to legal issues and risks, your organization is probably already doing this. Organizations should provide training to first- and second-line supervisors over a reasonable time frame, and as budgets allow. Some of the subjects that need to be addressed here are workplace diversity, harassment problems, and proper evaluations of employees. Employee survey results, exit interviews, or any incidents of related employee complaints and/or legal action may indicate areas in which supervisors need to be trained.

Incurring expense for training may seem unnecessary, but it can serve as an insurance policy. Training may prevent actions that could be possibly threatening to the organization's existence. And the results of quality training should result in smoother operations for your organizational culture. Training expense is surely justified.

Quality of Work Life Assessments

Quality of work life (QWL) assessments could be viewed as the large company level version of the employees' declarations that an organization is truly employee friendly.

A QWL assessment does not have to be exotic or complicated to get the job done. QWL assessments can be done in house with your existing personnel. These assessments are intended to be tools for you to grade how effectively your organization has transformed into a truly employee friendly workplace. The main points here are for the assessments to be done at intervals not to exceed three years, and the results be reported to upper management. The information is a report card on how effective the organization has been.

Upper management will be scrutinizing the cost-effectiveness of measures taken. As every effort has been taken to assure justification and positive bottom-line impact in designing these criteria, the CEFW program should pass upper management's scrutiny easily.

Fine-tuning and customization of the criteria for each organization is suggested and encouraged.

Any positive comments about the CEFW program should be reported in your organization's newsletter to demonstrate upper management commitment and support. Such demonstrations are necessary to keep interest high and maintain momentum. Every three years is a very lenient requirement and, depending on your individual program and how dynamic your organization is, QWL assessments may need to be done more often.

Alternative Dispute Resolution

It is suggested, but not required for certification, that your organization implement some sort of Alternative Dispute Resolution (ADR) program. ADR programs were created with the intent of protecting both the organization and its employees from the distractions of unresolved disputes and/or litigation while maintaining a fair and reasonable means of resolving the conflicts. Contact a firm that specializes in ADR to check for changes in laws and practices, and to be sure that ADR is right for your organization before committing to it.

Comp Time

It is suggested, but not required for certification, that your organization allow time-off compensation in lieu of overtime pay for employees that want it. So-called "comp time" is often preferred by employees, because they have personal errands and other business to deal with while maintaining full-time employment. Other employees who work long hours would just like some time off to be with their friends and family. Some pending legislation may affect comp time, so be sure to check on the current status before setting a policy that may conflict with any new laws. If you are awarding comp time in lieu of overtime pay, it would be considered proper to award it at the same rate (one and one-half times number of hours compensated for) as you would overtime pay. Your employees should be given the choice of pay or comp time to be fair for those who do need or want the extra money. Please note: currently comp time is only allowed for employees working in the public sector, but as of this writing, there are proposals to change this situation.

CHAPTER THREE

Contact Information for the Manager

Pursuing Excellence in Employee Relations

The Association for Quality and Participation (AQP):

AQP is a non-profit organization advocating the integration of quality and participation practices in all workplaces and communities. They can be reached at:

Association for Quality and Participation

P.O. Box 2055

Milwaukee, WI 53201-2055

Phone: 800-733-3310

Fax: 513-381-0070

www.aqp.org

Greenwich Institute For American Education (I-Power):

They are a non-profit corporation. They conduct seminars across the country and sell newsletters and books relevant to their flagship employee involvement program called "I-Power". It is a very simple but effective entry-level employee involvement program. A newsletter called *I-Power News* is also available. They can be contacted at:

Greenwich Institute for American Education/ Boardroom, Inc.

281 Tresser Blvd. 8th Floor

Stamford, CT 06901-3246

Phone: 203-973-6226

Fax: 203-967-3068

www.i-power.com

The Employee Involvement Association (EIA):

This group has been around for a long time and was formally called the National Association of Suggestion Systems. They not only provide services to members related to employee involvement programs, but also collect data relevant to savings from such programs. A recent report stated that member organizations were saving five dollars for every dollar spent on employee relations programs. Several different certifications are available through EIA for professionals who administer and manage employee involvement programs. They can be contacted at:

Employee Involvement Association

525 S.W. 5th Street, Suite A

Des Moines, IA 50309-4501

Phone: 515-282-8192

Fax: 515-282-9117

www.eia.com

Institute of Management Consultants (IMC):

The IMC is a national organization that certifies management consultants. They are a good resource to find competent management consultants to help you improve your organization. Their web site is useful and easy to use. IMC can be reached at:

Institute of Management Consultants

2025 M Street N.W. Suite 800

Washington, D. C. 20036-3309

Phone: 202-367-1134

Fax: 202-367-2134

www.imcusa.org

The Society for Human Resource Management (SHRM):

SHRM is a large organization devoted to all aspects of Human Resources and Employee Relations management. They keep members up to date on the latest employment laws and have a huge amount of critical resources. They certify HR professionals, have chapters in most populated areas of the U.S., and maintain a very popular web site. Contact them at:

Society for Human Resource Management

1800 Duke Street

Alexandria VA 22314

Phone: (703) 548-3440

www.shrm.org

These are just a few to get you started. You are urged to look on the Internet for other resources and latest addresses and contact information on the above resources as they move and evolve. Many other management organizations have ties to employee involvement and employee relations also, since a good employee relationship is essential for business success.

CHAPTER FOUR

Here is a Good Example of an Employee

Opinion Survey

The questions in this survey example were designed to reveal as much information as possible. The one to ten scale that is used on many questions may at first seem simplistic, but it allows scores to be easily understood. The one to ten scale can also be used to quickly check individual surveys for disgruntled employees. It is suggested, of course, that any employee survey should be customized to the individual company for maximum benefit.

SAMPLE EMPLOYEE SURVEY

INSTRUCTIONS: Indicate your answers to the following questions in the spaces provided. Please answer as honestly as possible.

1. _____ How would you rate the services that <the company> provides to its clients?

> (1 to 10 scale, 10 = best service)

2. _____ How would you rate the overall working conditions at <the company>?

> (1 to 10 scale, 10 = best conditions)

3. _____ How safe do you consider your job is against layoffs?

> (1 to 10 scale, 10 = most safe)

4. _____ Currently, what is your level of overall satisfaction with your job?

> (1 to 10 scale, 10 = most satisfied)

5. _____ How would you rate the quality of the company equipment you work with?

> (1 to 10 scale, 10 = highest quality)

6. _____ How stressful is your job?

> (1 to 10 scale, 10 = most stressful)

7. _____ How would you rate the company for overall fairness and equal treatment of employees?

(1 to 10 scale, 10 = most fair)

8. _____ How satisfied are you with the current system of employee evaluation to let you know how well you are performing your job?

(1 to 10 scale, 10 = most satisfied)

9. _____ How would you rate the chances of advancement within your company?

(1 to 10 scale, 10 = highest chance)

10. _____ Overall, how effective do you believe the management team of your company is?

(1 to 10 scale, 10 = most effective)

11. _____ How would you rate your company's ability to communicate important information to its employees?

(1 to 10 scale, 10 = highest ability)

12. _____ How would you rate the benefits package provided to you by your company?

(1 to 10 scale, 10 = best benefits)

13. _____ How would you rate your pay at <the company>?

(1 to 10 scale, 10 = best)

14. _____ How approachable is your supervisor when you take a problem to him or her?

(1 to 10 scale, 10 = most approachable)

15. _____ How would you rate the concern your company has for you as a human being?

(1 to 10 scale, 10 = most concern)

16. _____ How would you rate your working relationship with your fellow employees?

(1 to 10 scale, 10 = best relationship)

17. _____ How satisfied are you with the effectiveness of the company's safety training program?

(1 to 10 scale, 10 = most satisfied)

18. _____ How comfortable are you with your knowledge and understanding of the company's policy and procedures book?

(1 to 10 scale, 10 = most comfortable)

19. Where do you think your company will be in 10 years? Circle One:

    Larger   Smaller   About the Same   Unsure

20. Do you feel that the management of your company is interested in employee suggestions? Circle One:

    Yes   No   Undecided

21. As far as you know, do you plan to stay with this company until retirement? Circle One:

    Yes   No   Undecided

22. Has your loyalty to the company increased or decreased in the last two years?

    Circle One: Increased   Decreased

    Why?_____

23. Are you clear about your job description?   In other words, are you clear about which of the various tasks at your work location are actually your responsibility? Circle One:

    Yes   No   Undecided

24. Do you believe that the company appreciates extra effort on the job?

   Yes   No   Undecided

25. Do you know what your company's main goals for the future are?

   Yes   No   Undecided

26. If you could change one thing at <the company>, what would it be?

   _____

CHAPTER FIVE

How to Obtain Certified Employee Friendly Workplace Certification for Your Organization

CEFW status is an award intended for those organizations that go the extra mile to proactively manage their relationship with employees. These organizations should have something to show for those efforts and to aid in attracting the best employees.

Any management consultant can check criteria met and declare a company as an employee friendly workplace. The CEFW and the criteria discussed in this book were developed by Spence Consulting. Spence Consulting, therefore, is fully prepared to work with your company and check criteria for a nominal fee. A handsome wood and brass plaque declares a company a certified employee friendly workplace.

Obtaining workplace certification is not intended to be intrusive, difficult, or complicated. It does provide a means to determine that the organization is truly employee friendly and is not just giving lip service to the idea of having a win-win relationship with its employees.

The CEFW criteria are under constant revision and have some built-in flexibility to accommodate unusual business circumstances. The bottom line is that if your organization follows the criteria in both word and intent, you should have no problem becoming certified.

Steps to Obtaining CEFW Certification:

Contact the author through his listing under (John W. Spence, CMC) on the Institute of Management Consultants web site at www.imcusa.org or through the publisher.

Index

About the Author

John W. "Wes" Spence learned about employee relations by studying companies that have had histories of problems with their employees. By analyzing problems he saw that were common to companies, he created a general solution known as "Certified Employee Friendly Workplace". He has held positions ranging from technical professional and Operations Manager, to Human Resources Director. Mr. Spence is an honor graduate of Lamar University and a graduate of the State University of New York. He is a Certified Management Consultant (CMC), and a Senior Professional in Human Resources (SPHR). Through his leadership, Mr. Spence has become known for practical solutions to the HR and employee relations problems that cost businesses huge sums of money annually.

www.ingramcontent.com/pod-product-compliance
Lightning Source LLC
Chambersburg PA
CBHW030358290526
45785CB00004B/1812